Na'im Ezghoul was born on June 7, 1964, in the city of Anjara, Jordan. After finishing school, he pursued his studies, earning a doctorate degree in India. His first attempt at writing poetry was at the age of 21 in 1986. It was never a work intended for publication or to be counted on as of significance. As a song, it was written mainly for the musical effects of its words not for the message that it might deliver. However, it turned out to be a love song in which both music and meaning work together for some level of musicality and warmth. The song: 'You Are the Fountain of My Life':

You are the fountain of my life,
You are the light by which I can carry on my life.
Without you the world is misty, cloudy, and dark.
I've been created in this world
Not to be separated from you,
But to be mixed: flesh, blood and one heart
Pulsing, giving musical feelings,
Amusing the mingled soul.

His early poems were particularly love and lyrical pieces, which showed a strong desire to express his personal emotions and feelings. Then, he was drawn to reflect on themes like the large-scale scientific development, especially the advent of the computer, with all the negative effects it could have on the working forces particularly the spiraling rate of unemployment and inflation as envisaged in those days. Moreover, Na'im became more obsessed with the potential negative influence of science in general on man's emotional growth, maturity, and moral integrity as a human being.

I dedicate this work to my wife, Shahenaz, who has always been there at my side, ready with supportive ideas and suggestions.

I also dedicate it to my daughters Razan and Rawan, and to my son Mohammed. They have helped me with designing and drawing the cover.

Na'im Ezghoul

MISCELLANY

POETRY AND DRAMATIC SKETCHES

AUSTIN MACAULEY PUBLISHERS™

LONDON • CAMBRIDGE • NEW YORK • SHARJAH

ISBN – 9789948044086 – (Paperback)
ISBN – 9789948044093 – (E-Book)

Application Number: MC-10-01-9342777
Age Classification: E

Printer Name: iPrint Global Ltd
Printer Address: Witchford, England

First Published 2022
AUSTIN MACAULEY PUBLISHERS FZE
Sharjah Publishing City
P.O Box [519201]
Sharjah, UAE
www.austinmacauley.ae
+971 655 95 202

Coronavirus Speaks to the World

Microscopic COVID-19,
Wreaking havoc in the world.
Super-nano in size; cosmic in action.
Big powers brought to their knees,
Pleading for mercy; pleading for release.
The COVID-19's clutch on the world with its nano hands;
As if through God's hands it plies.
It brings the whole world to speak its tongue,
Its law and rhythm to follow, its melody to sing.
The world's motion is being slowed,
Its rhythm staggering with death in control.
It is a coup in disguise; power devolved swiftly in no time.
It's a game with coronavirus outplaying man.
Racking up a chain of points and an upper hand.
Man's claim to superiority is marred.
Wisdom is not measured with power, do you understand?
It is the law of the creator – it's nobody's private world;
It's nobody's private world.

A New World System

Corona flipping around man's everyday life details,
Re-orchestrating the parts, splitting up the unified,
Rolling out a new system, a new hierarchy in sight.

Corona is not a flash of light in an underground tunnel,
It is more, it is a spark that started the fire.
In a dry world where love and humanity fled,
It is a world fueled with hatred, stained with greed.

It's a super-nano spirit girdling the world,
Leaving man muddled and confused.
A blacked-out world with science standing inert,
A super-nano organism begetting a new world.

Magic seems to supersede and science to succeed;
Every corner around the world by ignorance ruled,
Waiting for Corona to take the lead.

Spiritual Crisis

Being materialistic to the bone,
Man panics at the sight of a loss;
Playing down spiritual failings and spiritual ebbs,
Highlighting material gains over feelings.

What he does not touch and sense,
It has no weight on his heart,
Being callous and unfeeling, he hates
With unwavering thrust.

Given to loathing, he flounders through love,
Like a toddler unsteady in its toddling steps
Takes pride at having a dying heart,
And at smothering the sparkling light.

To him love is such an abandoned feeling,
Outworn and beyond repair.
It is not worth the effort, not worth the pain,
As long as it has no material benefits in return.

Life along the material line
Sucks up man's inner being,

Leaving him empty, living only through a voice,
Through a shiny, waning crust.

Eternity

There and nowhere else dreams are so real!
Time flows into timelessness;
Into eternity they crescendo reach.
Into a spiritual mating they make it to the peak.
So tuned and seamless their breath and speech.

The dream world conquers that of Time
Among arresting, cliffs, rivers, and eye-catching mountains,
Nature renames the clock's time while marching,
To segue into Nirvana, into the world of Being.

Nature checks time as it passes into a trance,
And yields to the sublime,
Eternity the timeless space,
Where time's laws surrender to nature's unfailing charms,
Only to give way to free blessings as it strides.

Sprinkled with a spiraling dreamy sphere,
Time is held spellbound; it fell asleep.

A Lyric on Youth

Youth stays fresh in memory.
Its freshness outclasses age and calculations;
It's a dream that switches from fantasy to reality back to dream again,
It is an idea that fights for recognition;
More, it's self-assurance with a dream riding stance.
I am a star in heaven – can you not see?
I am the knight who toured the Earth and to another planet can flee;
I am somebody so distinct like nobody else can be;
I can fetch the moon and make it revolve around me;
I can travel at light speed, and where all fail, I am the one who succeeds;
I can be true to falsehood and the impossible more than a phoenix can;
I can give a truer face to the faceless nothing
Than a dragon can actually appear with a true face.
I like the myth that propels and stretches to the limit the impetus in us.
It's the force that sharpens and makes our aging more meaningful and sensible.

Yet, youth is more of a truth than a truth every one of us can draw.

It's a common property that we can make of it
What one can and what another cannot of it make.
It's a tree which, if cultivated right, can look great and so bright.

The Heart Once…!!!

The heart once the temple of love.
Now an abandoned house for abundant vile.
It had once leaching walls that for love cried.
Of misuse it has turned out to be
A pumping machine for a robot.

Man happened to be a creature that loved
For love and for love hated too.
He has turned out to be a hater of love
And hates for self-interest too.
It's now: man's heart is his swelling bank account;
The archetypal one is only a retired part.
The new just sustains the machine against falling apart.

Now man's heart outside him lies;
Hunting for happiness, success and triumph,
Away from that glorious past;
Into a meaningless future, edging collapse.

A Lyric on Truth

Truuuuuth, truuuuth, truuuuth…!!!
Has departed to an unknown place,
Agitated by evil which burns and burns every stone
That seems to truth akin.
Love must a chameleon mock to survive,
But does love have the love it should give
When the chameleon within it trapped?
True love to stay must swallow dross:
Truth must speak with a twisted tongue,
It must be exiled and not be heard from;
It must live the hermit's life and sleep undisturbed.
It must look from far and say no word.
To live, it must join hands with evil,
But can truth sustain truthfulness with evil's aid?
Alas! Today's truth versions march across the devil's land
Carrying the devil's seal, and with it, they are stamped!

The Unconscious

Dreams, hunters in deadly dark seas,
Of truth abruptly spotted.
How come darkness guidance gives?
It is how darkness natural light distills.
Processed truths fail to deliver fitting plans,
Where a caesarian labor retains the scar.

Man's true self lies in a world deep within,
Secluded from the tides and ebbs of time,
Into timelessness unharnessed as it strides.

Moments of truth spark up in dreams;
Slips of tongue deciphering do not need:
Sparkle in the depth of man's self,
Delivering light that never wanes.

Man's manufactured truths born into light,
Instantly grow dimmer and less bright.
They are gamed and weighed on a win-lose scale,
Mind games displaying a fleeting pride.

Our Time

Journeying down the time scale up to ours,
Each generation has a collective note ladder,
Ours the most supersonic so far:
With time curtailed to minimum at every activity,
With hours, days, years' fast pacing strides,
Predictable rules, suspended, overtaken and replaced;
Tortoises, being out of sync, lagged behind.
Our eyes, ears and hearts
Stopped ruling as archetypes;
Aided to reach the remotest corners in a flash.

A Song

Truly I love you!
More than I can do.
Beyond all horizons and depths,
I do love you!
My love to you
Exceeds the physical, the emotional
To unite with **Love**
In its heavenly hue.

Spring But...!

Flowers quiver, not dance,
Embracing out of fear time's indifference.
With suspended joy, they receive
Spring's prime times of the year.
Withdrawn into the shimmering flights of the night.
Into a deferred present, into a future winter flight.

Severed of their archetype:
Flowers, sickly they are. Hallucinated by broken dreams;
By the devil's happy and close bond with man.
Deflating what was once the crowning flowery tower.
Whose off springs are these quivering flowers.

The Broken Mirror

Travelling across the horizon, obscured into that far end,
Truth is degrading and reduced to a thin state.
In a world where breathing does not mean life,
Where the absence of it proves not death,
Ambiguity speaks and is understood;
Tears seem creatures from nowhere,
Speaking nobody's tongue.
They have become mostly extinct;
They exist in a different form and substance.
They mean something they never meant.
It is how our emotions become fossilized and blunt.

Success

Life hardly flourishes without toiling and dolour,
Cakewalks effect not what one aspires:

The grammar of love in hatred born,
And that of happiness in sorrow thrown.
Nothing without its inherent opposite code
Has enough reason to hone.

Dreams grow out of reality,
Reality out of dreams flows.
Hope slows on solid grounds,
It picks greater force on thinning ropes.

Truth blurs in sunshine,
In the abyss of dark, light is traced.
What is missing turns the wheels.
Man being in a permanent lack,
Perfection forever tracks.

Peace

The human ethics, once an ever-lovely lyric,
Sings of peace, harmony, and success.

Now, we over brood over scientific questions
Which accelerate life wheels,
Hardly gives us any scope to feel,
But dries up that stream of life
With all the reasoning limitations.

The concrete we see, we sense;
The inner forces if no more exist,
We are left with one rigid force
And forced to follow one single course.
Now, it is so, man is possessed by the material;
His reason throbbing in his muscles.

Let us look forward to the future's space
And fill it up with emotions and feelings,
But take care not to dry it up again.
Let reason and feelings stride along
To balance mistakes and brand them human.
Let us call peace human question

And warring below man's phylum.

Let us give poetry the chance,
And human evil shan't succeed
Though evil shall always exist, it shall never ahead proceed.
Let us synthesize to dilute intensities
And break the hard facts into human peace.

Pollution

Pollution is a scientific term,
It was born in a scientific stream.
Science dreamt of begetting civilization,
It got with uncertainty and new fashions.
It delivered pollution and contamination.
Science came to raise us high
And throw us down to die.
Uncertainty as its first child,
Colored with illusion and pride.

New frames introduced to face new terms:
Every idea came to a different claim.
Computers came to raise the people's flame,
The term inflation is born
To claim science to be blamed.
Exploitation came as a customs station,
Workers created associations for demonstration,
Airplanes, army equipment, nuclear and atom bombs
Introduced to reduce the flux of population.

Thanks to science –
It probes into well-felt balance:

It constructs and destructs,
It is like a mad man
Who, when finds nothing to do,
Turns back to ruin his being true.

Our Star

Admiring the oval shape,
Cutting it into beams: one love applies to all.
Alas! Demarcations dance in the concrete
On the contours of our breath and our speech.
The oral voice is our only choice
To make better the divided human race.

No doubt, our life is sparsely
Punctuated with holistic verbal touches, and
When in Nirvana fall.
These dreamy romantic fables
Can nurture positively our global bonds.
Such timeless and dreamy flights
Can balance our conscious biased strife.
And bring about a change of heart.

A Lyric on Drugs

Can you venture to play with a gun with yourself as an aim?
Can you venture to jump through a huge blazing flame?
Venturing into drugs is the same type of a game;
Venturing into drugs brings an endless pain.

Youth is a treasure not exchangeable for a fleeting whim,
Youth is a grace and power that never slims,
Youth is a massive propelling machine
That powers our life with a life unseen.
So, let not drugs into our life creep.

Let's whisper into our juveniles' ears a piece of advice
That doing drugs is a serious vice;
Let's show enough paternal affection
To help them find the right direction.

A Lyric

Acupressure is a treasure;
It absorbs pain with pleasure;
It is a costless play,
No tablets to swallow and costs to pay.
Just fondle yourself all the way,
And pains shall sneak away.
It is like a lullaby that sends you to sleep.

On a foggy day of your soul
When the body goes foggy all in all;
Although sleep is a natural relief,
Acupressure outclasses all healing styles.

The Other

Things co-exist in total harmony;
In total discord man does:
Color for man has a rank and a stand.
Do we choose the given, or the given choose us?
More, it is all about skin that adds nothing to a human,
If it hatred and division adds.

Racism, a sleeping devil awakened by hate,
A masked monster with everything fake;
A timed bomb of unspoken words and of actions held back.
Time comes when spiraling words and actions hurt;
On board day light, defying rules.
Are we typecast for certain roles in life,
And color and race make guilty or innocent our case?
How can one be right all the time being of a certain color?
And be wrong all the time for being of another?
It's racism awakened from a slumber,
It never goes into deep sleep.
It is always on the watch behind unspoken words;
In abeyance held, waiting to rebel.

A Song of Welcome

Take your seats;
Smile, be cool and confident.
Before all, sow your seeds of success,
Then plant your heart with love for all.
Charge your life with motivation
To take you to the next station.
For life is a string of stations,
And crossing from one to another needs motivation.
Motivation with hope is the fuel
Without which you miss being cool.
Charge your life with motivation;
Do not miss out on planning.
Charge your life with motivation.

A World That Cannot See

The world sees and does not,
Cannot see and does not want.
Politicians hide behind hideous and criminal claims,
Talk about humanity using inhumane terms.
Manipulation is the language of the perjurers,
It is used to prove the false true.
It is modern democracy that gives the devious the right to speak
About what's right and what's not, putting on Mother Teresa's mask.

Innocents are being killed before the eyes of the so-called civilized world;
They are being offered as sacrifices at the devil's altar
To appease the devil's pride.
It's why the world is silent and tongue-tied,
Paying only lip-service to the oppressed.

The warfare agents speak one language that is of war;
They wage wars everywhere both silent and declared
Against the right which they claim to be wrong;
Against humanity and the morally good.

The Liquidation of the Good

It seems to be the case that Good and Evil have struck a deal
To let go what does not in normal cases do.
It is the coalition between the two that makes the good, evil
too.
It is our time, the present, when everything around is gray.

Evil is the lawyer; evil is the judge.
The right is drowned and the wrong is crowned;
You hug with force who you hate of course.

It is a world siding with evil in its dominating course.
Masks prevail and approval granted,
Being plain is a matter of disdain.
Trickery is the art of love and living.
Directness and honesty is no less than a coup,
Which undermines and mars life's colorful hues.

Hopes

The train, alas! Went forever,
Only hopes live on,
Let us not lean much upon,
For life needs more than hoping.

Actions sweep away life's cloudy days
And give life a genuine and realistic look,
Although hope and dreaming spice up one's life,
They never spice to life give.

Actions in actual day-to- day life set things in stone,
Whereas hopes and dreams flickering and eventually fade.
They at times spur actions and at others foil them
When the thick clouds of life hide the sun.

Man and Change

Here we stand crippled,
Stagnant and with little hopes.
With crutches everywhere to take us around,
Man has grown into an unfeeling stone.

In this world where flowers grow,
Where spring comes to go,
All must move to see,
Man has opted to be something new.

Where nature goes in a cycle man breaks the rules
Unforeseen his actions, unforeseen his inventions.
With science he reversed the rules and dried the souls.

A natural waterfall climbs down as it goes;
The electric one points up with unnatural flow.
The movement up is not nature's;
Instinct never nature betrays
As it takes only one single way.

If gravity has anything to say,
It says it always in the same way.

If man has anything to say,
He says it in one-hundred-and-one different ways.

Politics

Down the street,
It is a big crowd,
Politicians race in rhetoric,
Forgetting what they say the next moment.
Nebulous is their way,
Fight peacefully to the public they say!

Politicians in political rings dance
At the worst of any situation expect a lucky chance;
They always a point make
That gives them more than from them takes.
Their words reflect paradise;
They project order as in the world of art.
As they take over power,
Begin to overlook facts in their ivory tower
And say the low should still be lower.

Politics is the art of manipulation,
Words swiftly arranged,
Like a propaganda on an opening newspaper page.
Words smoothly run
And everyone their only one meaning learns.

In our everyday dreams,
Thinking of politics –
We invite history to give its lesson:
Politics never to anyone listens.
It talks of desires that sets its owners on fire
And moves them to meet crowds.

Alas! The public always fail to realize,
As they fall under politicians' spell,
Politicians know the game very well,
They play back magic songs,
They gather around them huge throngs,
All realize the false true
The anti becomes pro.
They cheat you, my dear, they cheat you!
I would say at the end
Among the many you choose,
The least that intends the public to fool.

A Big Loss

O, Rajiv, nobody believes
You are no more!
I gaze in newspapers,
Your political image expresses loyalty to the soil,
Your smile shows a heart with the people,
And a mind devoted to their service.

The man whose interest in politics was not there,
Intended to serve his people with care.
Politics for him is a line
Drawn by his great great grandfathers –
Non-violence, love, peace, and harmony;
He held them all as the base for
Integrity, development, and prosperity.
O, Rajiv, nobody believes you are no more!

Your murder remains a stain in the assassin's life,
In this event, India suffered a loss too huge to repair.

Decisions

Never opt for the smooth and easy;
Life is not so very breezy.
Our options should define
Adoptions of facts and reason.

All beauties share this one fact:
They vanish against their will.
Soft options go to despair;
They disappear unheeded.

Rational decisions have a staying power,
They chisel our existence into a fulfilled plan
Into happiness, limned and engraved by our hands.

The Almighty's Will to Man

Ahmed: The world doesn't seem to be what it normally was, does it?

Faisal: You're about right, but it's not a de facto shift that the world experiences. However, the shift is more a reflection of a new level of perception and evolution in science which the modern man experiences, affecting the way we see the world, not the world per se.

Hussam: Exactly, man has skipped the true version of reality to focus on the virtual reality and realities which science presents. Man's natural potential has been undervalued for the logic of science which is, for the most part, hard and dry.

Ahmed: Yes, it is. Man has excelled as an inventor of new devices, not to find out truth, but to mystify it, with an eye on disturbing and falsifying the Truth created by Allah. However, Allah's logic is far beyond the scope of the human mind to understand. Therefore, Allah's truth is Allah's Will to all humanity. It's definitely different from man's style of deducting truth through material devices. For instance, Love as created by Allah functions as a unifying force. It works towards bringing humanity together. However, it is actually twisted by man's uneven list of exclusions on several bases.

Faisal: I second what you say. The bright outward look of the world is only a deception. It's a nice smelling poison that kills silently. Science and material success have taught us to love ourselves the most and do so little to love others. Thus, selfishness is man's scheme, whereas Allah's scheme is for all and annoys none. Allah's plan is holistic: it is Truth, Justice and Mercy. It suffers from no deficiency. It is intact, comprehensive, and whole.

Mutuality Versus True Love

Hadi: I woke up in a dream where love is the air we breathe, and who ceases to love ceases to live.

Faris: O, what a dream it is! If it turns out to be a reality, then it'll have the deadly effect of a nuclear bomb.

Hadi: How's that?

Faris: With too much callousness and indifference in today's world, life on Earth has lost much of its vigor and beauty.

Saeed comes in and gives Faris a big hug.

Saeed: What a happy coincidence! It seems to be that chance meetings give life a better taste than planned ones! What's it you are here about in the early morning?

Hadi: Nothing much, Faris is back from a journey abroad.

Faris: Eventually, it's all about simplicity. If you unlock your mind and heart, you'll be free of all that might tantalize you.

Saeed: So, do you want to tell me that you've also met by chance?

Hadi: Yes, but more than that is the lasting friendly relationships which count more, not the ones which hinge upon a goal or determined by a benefit.

Saeed: What do you mean?

Hadi: The true test for loyalty in friendship is perseverance and dedication in the face of all adverse and unfavorable conditions.

Saeed: Yes, I can see! connections and intimacy among friends has a great magnetic force which makes friends stay in a spinning move in their orbits around friendship.

Hadi: Yeah, it goes without saying – love is one of the most relieving of the human emotions which humanity should value the most, and only an antihuman will have a different say. What do you think?

Faris: Whoever love does not improve, will have the devil as a friend.

Saeed: Yes, it is. Today's world is replete with relationships and connections built on the mutual exchange of interests, conducing unfortunately to a high degree of mistrust. Such relationships largely build uneven bridges among individuals on the basis of reciprocity which pay not more than a lip service to love and human rapport. It, on the contrary, spreads the evil effects of mutuality into society, no more, no less.

Hadi: Exactly! And once people's interests are fulfilled, they part with one another tight-lipped. The bond between them is solely about the exchange of interests. Can mutuality in any real way help further human interactions beyond the limited material scope of dealings? To me, I'd say it does not add the least to the humanity of Man. On the contrary, it builds fences around the human heart and allows the mind to weave complicated, soulless bonds based on transactions and fiscal dealings.

Saeed: Unfortunately, in today's world, the power of mutuality has exceeded all limits. Therefore, creating connections and relationships in a traditional way has really become off-pace in this material world where we live. We are, it is to say, in a world guided by the devil after undermining human values for material gains.

Hadi: Do you mean to back out of love as the central emotion and medium for a healthy existence? Or is it another way to express your submission to the material way of existence?

Saeed: Never, never to me love is what it's always been, the main and leading drive that motivates those who rate humanity high. For the antihuman, love is not more than an unworthy emotion which deserves not to be heeded. The ideal solution for reversing the serious effects of mutuality could be to strike a balance between addressing human relationships on the basis of human affection and mercy and that of stipulating fair material dealings.

Hadi: Yes, you're right. A balanced handling of the issue of mutuality can really alleviate the negative effects of the extreme material interactions among people in general. If not, hatred will continue to make of the killing of innocents a kind of game. It'll persist in giving authority to evil over peace and love. It is indeed, the archenemy of life and a partisan for all types of adversity. It smiles at the sight of oppression and frowns at that of love.